Face to the Sky

Alba Ambert

Illustrated by Maya C. González

Rigby

© 1999 by Rigby
a division of Reed Elsevier Inc.
500 Coventry Lane
Crystal Lake, IL 60014

Executive Editor: Lynelle H. Morgenthaler
Design assistance provided by Herman Adler Design Group

04 03 02 01 00 99
10 9 8 7 6 5 4 3

Printed in Singapore

ISBN 0-7635-5712-9

Whenever Yanira longs
for the radiant sun of Puerto Rico,
she runs beyond the clattering swings
and the peeling seesaws of the brown-grassed park.
She runs to the top of the tallest hill,
clutching a telescope in her fist.

There, at the very top, where the cold wind
whistles and clouds huddle low,
she scans the sky with her telescope.
She wonders if her island friends
turn their faces to the sky,
to the twinkling stars
she likes to look at in the night.

When light drifts down
and shadows peek behind the hill,
Yanira rubs her eyes and heads home.
She looks out the window
to watch the sun drop to the ground
and thinks about the friends she left behind.

Tonight the sky is a dark blue velvet fabric
when Yanira looks out.
Through stars that scatter
like coins in the sky,
she sees the moon slice
the darkness like a sliver of silver.

As Yanira faces the milky beams of the moon,
its features scarred with dark shadows,
she is dazzled by the mystery of the skies
and wonders what the darkness hides
in the folds of the night.

7

The moon, a shiny rock pitted with craters,
spins round the Earth
while the Earth and other planets orbit the sun.
Yanira knows that the sun, big and hot,
is the center of the solar system, churning with waves
of bright gas and bursts of light.

8

Like a giant fireball, the sun hurls
her fiery heat and light to all the planets.
The sun is strong and pulls the planets toward herself
as they spin round and round like colored tops.
Yanira gazes at the sky and thinks
about each lonely planet
spinning alone in the velvet sky.

9

She finds Mercury closest to the sun.
Wrinkled with ridges,
he's like the skin of a dried apple.
Dark skies are all that Mercury knows.
He has no air to reflect sunlight,
so on Mercury the sky is always black.
In the daytime, the sun's rays flood Mercury with heat.
And he boils and he cooks and he's so hot
that lead could melt and flow
like water over rocks.
But every night when the sun is gone,
Mercury shivers with cold in his deserted darkness.

Venus is a gleaming pearl in the evening sky.
She lies with Mercury between the Earth and the sun
and is only seen at twilight
or just before the rise of the sun.
Shawls of thick, hazy clouds wrap around Venus
and trap the fiery heat of the sun.
A dusty carpet of lava plains
lies between her mountains and peaks.
Venus is hotter than Mercury, as big as the Earth.

On the planet Earth, next from the sun,
a hard rocky crust crests into
towering mountains and grumbling volcanoes.
Everywhere on Earth, there is water
to fill her vast oceans.
Air bathes the planet Earth,
and the sun shines over her.
Without the heat and light of the sun,
the Earth would be colder than snow,
colder than ice.

Once, millions of years ago,
when Mars was very young,
he wore a coat of iron.
But Mars was warm and damp then,
and his iron coat rusted with moisture.
The rust made Mars
blush red as a heart.
Now Mars whirls with strong winds
and kicks up huge dust clouds
that hide the deserts of rocks
that lie under his orange sky.
At night Mars chills and frosts.
Two small moons orbit Mars
like baseballs spinning in the air.

Giant Jupiter could fit
any of the other planets inside.
Jupiter spins so fast,
clouds shred into thin belts of color
and a slender ring circles him like a halo.
A vast whirlpool smudges Jupiter
with a big red spot.
But still Jupiter is beautiful
with his swirling clouds and wands of light.

Saturn seems calm and pale as he shows off
the beauty of his majestic rings and dazzling moons.
But every now and then a raging storm
blasts through and darkens him with thick splotches
beneath his circling rings.
But Saturn spins so fast, the splotches tear apart,
become specks,
and disappear.

Tiny bits of rock, ice, and dust
shape the slender rings of Uranus.
Uranus turns on his side
as his many moons,
sharpened with ice cliffs,
craters, and ridges,
gather speed and spin
like the balls of a juggler.

Neptune's blue veil
glimmers like smooth ice.
But the fiercest winds of all the planets
rip across Neptune while he spins one way
and the winds blow the other.
Neptune spins and spins
while the winds rip and roar through him.

21

Tiny Pluto is farthest from the sun.
Pluto swings around in space,
at times moving closer to the sun
and catching some of the warmth of her rays.
Other times, Pluto sweeps far away
and becomes a mantle of ice.

22

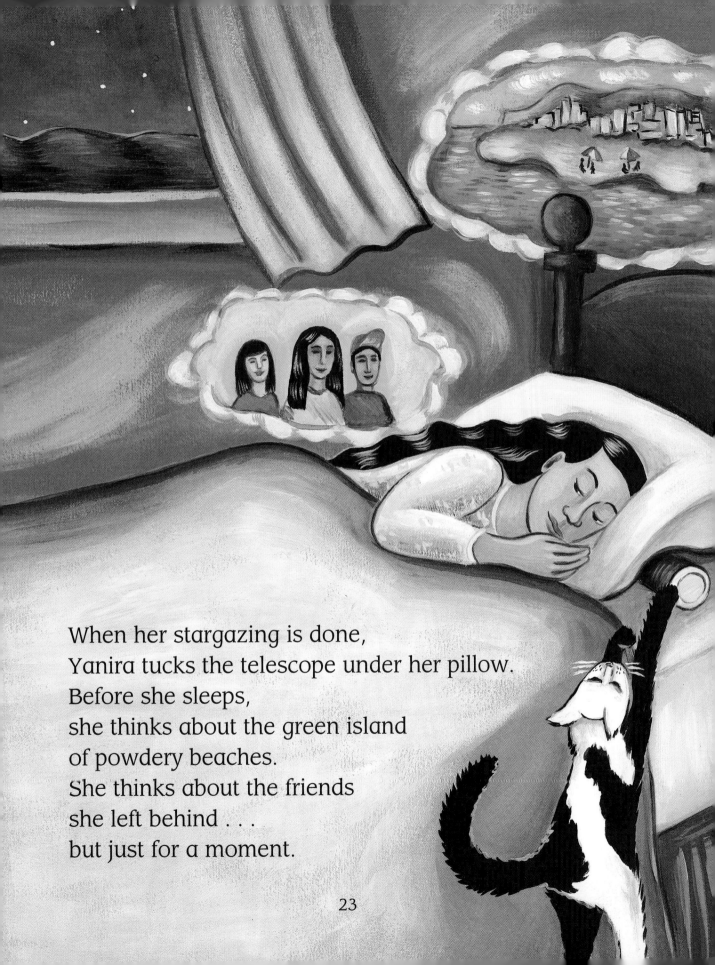

When her stargazing is done,
Yanira tucks the telescope under her pillow.
Before she sleeps,
she thinks about the green island
of powdery beaches.
She thinks about the friends
she left behind . . .
but just for a moment.

As she slips into her dreams,
Yanira takes flight
to the glowing sun,
the brilliant planets,
and the moons and rings
that swirl around them.